the Gerbil

A guide to selection, housing, care,
nutrition, behaviour, health, breeding,
species and colours

Contents

Contents

Foreword

This book has been written to provide the basic information that you need if you want to keep a gerbil as a
pet. Besides that, you will also find useful background
information and some interesting facts.
'The Gerbil' has been written as a book for beginning
and advanced enthusiasts and breeders.

Besides general issues, such as origin, selection,
purchase, feeding, housing, care and reproduction,
the hobby of small animal breeding is also covered.
Many gerbil breeders find this an exciting hobby.
A separate chapter is dedicated to other species of
gerbils. These are gerbils, which are closely related to
the Mongolian gerbil that is central to this book.
Many enthusiasts keep these other gerbils as pets also.

About Pets

A Publication of About Pets.

All rights reserved, including the right
to reproduce this book or portions
thereof in any form whatsoever.

ISBN 1852792132
First printing
September 2003

Original title: *de gerbil*
© 1999 - 2002 Welzo Media Productions bv,
About Pets bv,
Warffum, the Netherlands
www.aboutpets.info

Photos:
Rob Dekker,
Rob Doolaard,
and Kingdom Books

Printed in Italy

General

The Mongolian gerbil's Latin name is Meriones unguiculatus which means 'clawed hunter'. It is more closely related to the hamster than to the rat, although people often think it is the other way round.

Mongolian gerbil
(Meriones unguiculatus)

Origin

There are various types of gerbils. They are found all over the world, mostly in dry, infertile and sandy steppes. [In English prairie is almost never used except when describing North American grasslands.] Gerbils are found in North Africa, Russia, Iran, Turkey, Sri Lanka, India, Northern China and Mongolia. The Mongolian gerbil is the best known and the most suitable to be kept as a pet. The Mongolian steppes, the original habitat of the Mongolian gerbil, is a biotope with a strange, extreme environment. As only a few animals can cope with such an extreme environment, the Mongolian gerbil does not have many natural enemies. To escape from those enemies that do exist, such as snakes and birds of prey, the gerbil

has a highly developed jumping ability. This ability, which is also useful when a gerbil is attacked by others of its kind, is the result of very strong back legs. Gerbils have a number of characteristics that are typical of desert animals. They have fantastic hearing. They can also store a lot of water in their layers of fat cells and are very economic with the little water they get. Gerbils urinate very little, and they produce very dry droppings.

Contrary to many other desert animals, the gerbil is not primarily nocturnal. It does stay in its burrow during the hottest time of the day, but it has alternating periods of waking and sleep. It is active for a few hours, and then it sleeps again for a few hours. This cycle is also carried on in captivity. This makes the gerbil a very attractive pet, as you can also see it in action during the day.

History

The gerbil has a fairly short history as a pet. Twenty breeding couples were captured in Eastern Mongolia and Manchuria. These animals are regarded as the ancestors of the gerbils which are kept in captivity today. Approximately twenty years after these first captive animals had been domesticated, the first gerbils were taken to the US for research. There, it very quickly became apparent, that these were unique animals, which also made ideal pets. The gerbil is interesting and safe in both its behaviour and its appearance. It is exceptionally intelligent and quickly learns individual tricks. This makes the gerbil an amusing and fascinating pet for people who can give it time and attention.

Rodents

Gerbils are rodents and therefore mammals, just like humans, dogs and horses. Rodents actually form the largest group of mammals; of

Mongolian gerbil,
Canadian white-spot

all the species of mammals in the world, more than half are rodents. The best-known rodents are probably mice and rats, but in fact they come in all shapes and sizes. The largest rodent in the world is the Capybara, or "water pig", which can grow to over one metre long and weigh more than 60 kg. The tiny tot among the rodents is the African dwarf mouse, which is never longer than three centimetres. Between these extremes one finds the squirrel, the guinea pig, the porcupine, marmot, hamster and countless other rodent varieties. Contrary to popular opinion, rabbits and hares are not rodents. They are more closely related to hoofed animals, such as the goat. However, rabbits and hares do share one significant characteristic with the rodents; they have continuously growing front teeth without roots. Because rodents are constantly gnawing, they grind their front teeth down. Nature found a solution by having their teeth just keep growing. However rodents do run the risk of so-called "Overgrown teeth" and you can read more about that in the chapter on "Your gerbil's health". When choosing a cage or a hutch, remember that rodents have sharp teeth and can easily chew a hole in wood.

Family tree

A family tree (see page 9) can help to show the position that rodents occupy in the animal hierarchy. All existing animals were first divided into two groups: vertebrates and non-vertebrates. The vertebrates have hard body parts, such as bones and teeth, and are in turn divided in to five classes: fish, amphibians, reptiles, birds and mammals. The latter, of course, were named "the higher species".

The mammals class is again divided into various orders. There is the order of predators, which apart from bears and tigers also includes dogs and cats. The whales fall under a special order. Contrary to what many believe, these animals do not belong in the fish class because their young are born alive. The apes belong to the primate order, while a kangaroo comes under the marsupials. And rodents have their own order, in Latin called Rodentia (hence the English word "rodent"). As we already said, rabbits and hares are not classified as rodents, they have their own order, the Lagomorpha.

The rodent order is then divided into four sub-orders: mice, squirrels, porcupines and guinea pig species. All rats, mice, gerbils and (dwarf) hamsters belong to the sub-order of the mice.

This sub-order of the mice is then again divided into three super-families: real mice, dormice and jumping mice.

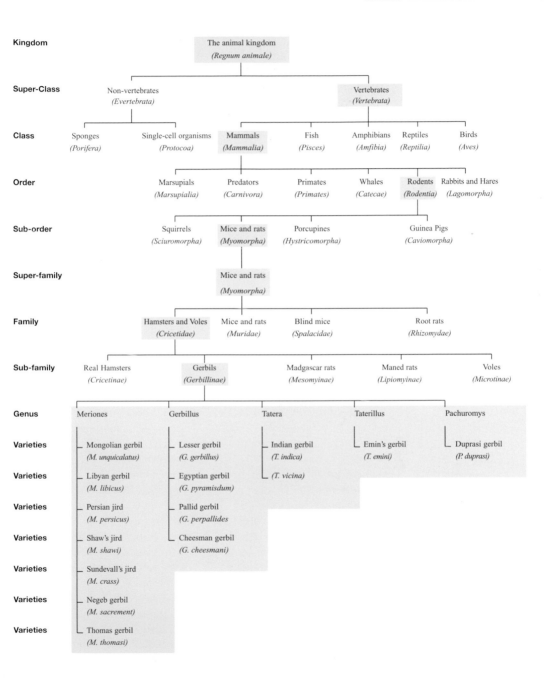

The super-family of the real mice is split into four families: hamsters and voles, mice and rats, root rats [I am not sure what a root rat is] and mole rats. Of course, mice belong to the mice and rats genus (Muridae).

The family of hamsters and voles has five sub-families: real hamsters, Madagascar rats, crested rats, voles and gerbils [you have used jumping mice above]. The Latin name for the last sub-family is Gerbillinae. The family of the jumping mice is divided into genera , such as (among others) Meriones, Gerbillus, Tatera and Taterillus. These genera are again divided into different tribes and species. You will find more about this in the chapter Special gerbils.

Physical characteristics

The Mongolian gerbil is a small animal. It is approximately twelve centimetres from nose to the base of the tail. Its furry tail adds another six to twelve centimetres. The male has a slightly sturdier posture than the female. It weighs between some 53 and 133 grams.
The gerbil's body is slim and has a tight skin. The head is short and wide, with a pointed nose.
The wild colour of the Mongolian gerbil (the so-called agouti) is achieved by a slate grey hair base, a yellow colour in the middle and a black top. The belly and the paws are beige to white. The coat should have a silky shine. This shine is the result of discharge from a gland on the belly. Both sexes have such a gland, with which they can spread their smell on objects and other animals of their kind. During the cleaning, they spread the substance, which contains pheromones (aromatic hormones), over their coat. Each gerbil has its unique smell, which helps the animals to identify each other. The gerbil's body temperature is between 37.4 and 39 °C. Its respiration rate is 70 to 120 per minute, and the heart beat is 260 to 600 per minute. Gerbils live for about three years, in some excep-

Lesser gerbil
(*Gerbillus gerbillus*)

tional cases they can reach the age of five. The underside of the female is slightly rounder, and the anus and the vagina are closer together than the male's anus and penis. You can see the scrotum at the base of the tail on an (almost) grown male.

Gerbils are often considered to be mice. There are, however, many differences between these two rodents. Gerbils dig holes, which mice do not. They both have shiny red or black eyes, but the gerbil's eyes are rounder and bigger. The gerbil's head is rounder and wider (like a squirrel's). Its back legs are longer than the front legs, whereas the mouse's legs are all the same length. Another unique characteristic of the gerbil is a small hairless spot on the otherwise completely fur-covered sole of the back paw. They also have a long, furry tail with a wisp of hair at the end. Mice have naked (hairless) tails. One difference that cannot be noticed at first sight is that the upper incisors of the gerbil have a groove lengthways, which is lacking on mice.

Buying a gerbil

Buying a gerbil need not be expensive. Young gerbils are often given away for nothing. However, you have to plan the purchase of a £3 (even the cheapest gerbil is unlikely to be less than £3) gerbil just as carefully as that of a very expensive pedigree dog.

Mongolian gerbil, black

Things to consider before buying

A small and fairly inexpensive rodent like the gerbil does involve some costs and effort. It needs a cage, food and care. Caring for one animal can cost (a lot) more time than another animal, but care is something that is needed every day, even when you come home tired from work or school, and during holidays. Before buying a gerbil, it's important to discuss this with the whole family. Anyone who plans to buy an animal should get as much information about it in advance. However sweet gerbils are, they do have their own needs in terms of care, food and environment. Discuss things with your family and ask yourself the following questions: Is a gerbil a suitable pet in your family situation? How intensive is the care it needs and do you have the time for it, over the long term? What does it eat, and what kind of cage does it need? Will you keep it alone or will it feel better in a pair or a group? How much is it going to cost to buy and care for (including vet's bills) and can you afford that? To avoid disappointments later, get the answers to these questions before buying your pet. In any event, don't be tempted by 'love at first sight', because buying on impulse is guaranteed to bring disappointment with your new pet later.

If you're buying a gerbil for a child, make solid agreements in advance about who is going to feed it and clean its cage. Practice shows that children often promise a lot in their enthusiasm, but don't always keep their promises over time. Don't expect too much, especially with very young children: they're certainly not old enough to take responsibility for a pet on their own. Before taking a gerbil home, be sure you've got proper accommodation for it (a cage, container or other accommodation). After all, you can't keep a rodent in a cardboard box.

What variety?

More than eighty species of gerbil are found worldwide. Only a small selection are kept as pets in this country. You can get to know about many of these in this book, in the chapter Other Species. Far less is known about keeping special gerbils than about keeping the Mongolian gerbil. If you do not have any experience in keeping rodents, it is easiest to start off with the common gerbil. More advanced gerbil enthusiasts can try their luck with more exotic types.

One or more?

The question as to whether to keep gerbils alone or together is very simple to answer. In the wild, some animals are social creatures and live in groups, families or as a pair. Other animals live alone, sometimes completely alone. They seek a mate to breed and then go their own way again. So it's important to keep animals that live alone in the wild alone in

captivity too. Animals that originally live in groups or as a pair are happier pets when they have a mate. Almost all gerbils are very definitely herd animals. They will feel very unhappy sitting alone in a cage. Gerbils may not be able to tell you about their mood in words, but they can certainly do so with their behaviour: a lonely gerbil will become listless and apathetic over time. If you are planning to keep gerbils as pets, you would be well advised to keep two or more animals of the same sex. There is then no risk of being overwhelmed with young, and, fortunately, it is easy for young gerbils to form groups. It is far more difficult to get adult animals used to each other as they can start vicious fights, which often end in one of the animals losing its life. In the chapter Reproduction you can find more on how to keep male and female adults together.

Where to buy

You have plenty of options where to buy a gerbil.

Most gerbils are sold by pet shops, which in itself is a good thing, as generally pet shop owners know how to look after the animals they sell properly.

However there are always some shops that are not so good. You can often spot what kind of a shop you're dealing with. Are the cages

Mongolian gerbil, polarfox

Mongolian gerbil, agouti

clean? Do all the animals have clean water? Are there too many animals in a small tank? Are they selling animals that are wounded or appear sick? Are the animals handled regularly?

Most pet shops obtain their rodents from enthusiasts or serious breeders. These animals are healthy and usually used to human hands.
Unfortunately, as well as serious breeders and animal lovers, we have our share of rogue breeders in this country. These are people who try to get rich quick by breeding as many gerbils, mice, rabbits or other pets as possible, often keeping the animals in disgusting conditions. They never, or hardly ever, take care of hygiene or animal welfare, and in-breeding is the order of the day. One of the major disadvantages of these "breeding factories" is that the young are separated from their mother far too early, because time is money after all. The young are nowhere near strong enough, and sooner or later become seriously ill. Never buy a gerbil (or other pet) that is still too young or too small.

However hard it may sound, never give in to the temptation to buy such an animal hoping to give it a better home. You're really not doing any good. The more animals these dealers can sell this way, the more they will

keep "in stock". They don't care why you're buying the animal, just as long as you buy it. But if nobody buys their tiny sick animals then they can't make any profit either, and they then have to decide either to stop trading or to start taking better care of their animals.

Things to watch out for

If you're planning to buy a gerbil, watch out for the following points:

• The animal must be healthy. A healthy gerbil has bright eyes and is lively. Sexual organs must be clean and the animal must not show signs of wounds or scars. Its coat must be smooth, clean and glossy. Look out for any lumps or swelling.

Mongolian gerbil, black

• The gerbil must not be too young or too small. During the first weeks of its life, the young animal gets resistance to disease through its mother's milk that is vital to its health.

• The animal must also not be too old. Gerbils have a relatively short life. Buying an older animal may mean you will only be able to enjoy it for a short period. Also, grown gerbils are more difficult to tame. You can recognise an older animal by its yellowish belly.

Mongolian gerbil, agouti

• Check whether your gerbil is really the same sex as the shop assistant tells you. Mistakes are often made on this point: two "females" often suddenly produce babies later.

• Make sure the animal is not too thin or too fat.

Mongolian gerbil, dove

Selling young gerbils

However much you like breeding gerbils, sooner or later you can't keep them all. Then you must sell, swap or give away the young.

You can sell young (and older) animals to a pet shop. In this case you never know where they will end up. In any event, look for a serious pet shop that provides broad and correct information when selling animals.

You can also sell the young to private individuals. You might notify a gerbil owners' club (see the chapter on Addresses), place an advertisement in the newspaper or, preferably, sell or give them to acquaintances. Always give the new owner(s) good information about feeding and caring for gerbils.

Whatever you do, never set animals free into the wild! They will certainly not survive.

Catching and handling

Animals that are not used to being picked up by human hands are always frightened by the experience. You can normally pick up your gerbil by lifting it from underneath. You put the other hand over it as a "lid" to prevent the animal from escaping. Young animals, especially, tend to jump off your hand in panic.

When animals are very wild (which is not usual with gerbils) you should use a jam jar to catch them. It is important to catch the animal as fast as possible. Although gerbils can normally cope well with stress, a long chase

can tire them out and cause them to go into shock. A gerbil in shock will lay flat on its chest with paws outstretched and make epileptic (jerking) movements.

Transport

When you buy, or are given, a gerbil, you have to get the animal home. In many cases this is done in a cardboard box. This is not the best solution. It would not be the first time (and won't be the last time either) that a gerbil gnaws a hole in such a box and goes off on a journey of discovery in the shopping bag or the car.

So it's better to get a transport container in advance, and you can buy one at any petshop. These containers are too small to be permanent housing, but very suitable for the first journey home or a trip to the vet's. You can also use it to house your animal temporarily when you're cleaning its cage.

Mongolian gerbil, silver agouti

But a disadvantage is that gerbils need a fair deal of bedding to dig around in. The base sides are usually low and a burrowing gerbil can easily throw sawdust over the edge.

Plastic or glass containers

Rodents are frequently kept in old aquariums or plastic containers with a wire gauze lid. In such a closed container the animals aren't bothered by draughts, but ventilation is not optimal. So you need to clean the cage litter frequently, otherwise the animals live in ammoniac fumes. A lid of glass or plastic sheet is absolutely out of the question because it allows no ventilation at all.

Plastic containers have the disadvantage that they quickly become unsightly, because they are easily scratched. The toilet corner in these containers can also become corroded and rough, making it difficult to keep clean and bad for hygiene.

Glass containers are available in various forms. One-piece containers

Thomas gerbil
(Meriones thomasi)

are easily kept clean, but are also heavy. And if one crack appears you might as well throw it away. There are also aquarium types with a metal frame holding panels of glass. In the past these panels were fixed with putty, which would, of course, not dry out when the aquarium was filled with water. However, old putty tends to crumble in a dry gerbil container. The animals can gnaw at it and the panels can become loose. So containers with putty are unsuitable. Nowadays, glass panels can be fixed with silicone, which is an easy job for any do-it-yourself enthusiast. You can also make a glass cage without a frame. The glass panels are glued together with silicon and after one day the container is so strong that you could actually fill it with water. This type of cage can easily and cheaply be made at home. The silicon bead should not be too thick, otherwise the animals will gnaw at it, and the corners should be polished smooth or protected with plastic corner strips, because they can easily cause injury.

Laboratory pen
Some people keep gerbils in a laboratory pen, [often advertised as simply a "lab pen"]. These are low plastic containers with a metal grille as lid. A laboratory container is ideal for housing a lot of animals with the minimum of work, which is the intention in a laboratory. But you have very litt- le contact with the animals. It is also questionable whether they feel happy in such a boring home, and some laboratory containers are so low that a gerbil can hardly stand upright inside it.

Gerbil paradise
Elaborate 'gerbil paradises' can be bought in pet shops. Some consist of a number of wired cages atta- ched to each other, others are a whole system of plastic tubes. Children, of course, find such an exciting gerbil house very attracti- ve. They are, however, not ideal. Some models have narrow tunnels and sharp edges. A gerbil with a full belly can easily become stuck. The tubes and burrows are also difficult to clean and the ventila- tion is bad. The biggest disadvan- tage is that gerbils can sink their teeth into the plastic and your gerbil paradise will look like Swiss cheese in no time.

Cage litter
For years, wood shavings have been used in animal cages. This is often called sawdust but is actually shavings. Sawdust absorbs moisture exceptionally well and hardly smells, but a disadvantage is that it usually con- tains a lot of dust. Investigations in recent years have shown that this dust can seriously bother rodents. There are now many other types of cage litter on the market that are "healthier" for animals.

Laboratory pen

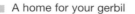

Sawdust

As we have said, sawdust is not especially suitable as cage litter. However, it does appear that animals like the gerbil, whose natural habitat is dusty and who like to burrow, are less affected by the dust in wood shavings. Nature has made them better at dealing with it. Now that the dust problem is generally recognised, some types of sawdust are cleaned better by the manufacturer. So wood shavings are ideal for your gerbil's home. They absorb plenty of moisture (a gerbil does not urinate very much) and they are great to dig and root around in. A layer of wood shavings mixed with hay (at least fifteen centimetres thick) is ideal to dig tunnels and burrows in. If the system collapses, the gerbil caught under it will be able to free itself without problems.

Hay

Rodents like to use hay as nesting material and to chew on, however it does not absorb moisture well and is thus not really suitable as cage litter.

Straw

Straw is much too coarse to be suitable as cage litter or nest material for rodents. There is a product on the market, which is made of shredded straw. Russell Rabbit cage litter is wonderfully soft and ideal as nesting material. It is less suitable as cage litter as it absorbs little moisture.

Cat litter

There are probably a hundred different sorts of cat litter on the market. Some are suitable to keep rodents on. Gerbils cannot really use litter made of stone or clay, as they cannot dig around in them.

Pressed pellets

Various cage litters are now on the market that consist of pressed pellets. Some types have sharp edges and don't seem very comfortable. They also fall apart when they become damp. Pellets made of plant material, such as maize, are a good alternative if your gerbil seems to be allergic to woodshavings. Symptoms of such an allergy are red eyes and a red nose. Maize pellets have the advantage

that they hardly ever contain chemicals, but the disadvantage is that the gerbil cannot really dig around in them.

Sand

Some rodents like to live on sand. But as a floor covering sand has the disadvantage that it doesn't store warmth and hardly absorbs moisture. Therefore sand alone is unsuitable for gerbils, but if you do choose to use it make sure there's good nesting material available in the cage. The sand also has to be completely dry. Only gerbil varieties from the Gerbillus family can live in a sand-only cage. They urinate so little that the moisture has evaporated before it reaches the bottom. Make sure, however, that you offer your gerbil a separate nesting area with suitable material.

Shredded paper

There are also various types of shredded paper on offer as cage litter. These shreds are ideal to play with and can be used as nest material. But they absorb much too little moisture to be used as cage litter.

Shredded paper

The interior

You can fill your gerbil's home with woodshavings and leave it at that. It would, however, be a very boring habitat, both for your gerbil and you. There are literally hundreds of different rodent toys in pet shops. Let's look at the advantages and disadvantages of a number of popular gerbil articles:

Gerbil houses

There are countless sorts of gerbil houses on sale, but most are made of plastic and will be gnawed to destruction within a very short time. Apart from that, most are too small. There are roomier versions, made of wood, which are more suitable for gerbils although they will also gnaw at these. You can also use a stone or glass pot. An empty package, such as a Cornflakes box, will also make a comfortable home. The gerbils will gnaw their out own door and windows. Once the house has been gnawed to destruction, you can replace it cheaply by a new one.

Wheels

Opinions vary on the usefulness of a wheel. Some people insist that these provide plenty of recreation for a gerbil. That's surely true, but on the other hand a wheel does force the animal into monotonous activity that may result in psychological disturbances. The fact is that gerbils would rather dig than run. When offered the chance to dig and shred, for example in woodshavings and with empty toilet rolls, they will not often use the wheel. If you do want to buy a wheel, choose a safe model with a solid running surface. This prevents your gerbil from becoming caught or losing its tail.

Straw houses

Gerbil houses, tunnels and balls made of straw have appeared on the market in recent years. These products are made of woven straw and hay held together by wire. These are ideal toys for gerbils! They can climb and tunnel in and around them and gnaw at the straw and hay. After a while the straw house is finished with and you just need to take the wire skeleton out of the cage.
[We have heard reports of these containing wire with dangerous sharp ends]

If you're not keen on ready-made plastic objects, you can fit out your gerbil's home really nicely with rocks and branches, giving it a pretty natural look. Make sure that the gerbils cannot easily reach the lid of the cage via the branches.Some gerbils love to gnaw at the bars for hours at a time, which can cause a dreadful noise, and make their noses sore. Also make sure that the branches are clean and no poisonous. Prunings from fruit trees that have not been sprayed should be safe.

The best place

Take care when picking the place to put your gerbil cage. Places where big temperature differences can occur, such as near an oven or radiator is not suitable, nor is a windowsill that is sometimes in full sunlight. Gerbils prefer a temperature of 20 to 24 °C. Although they are desert animals, they do not like extreme temperatures. In the wild, they withdraw into their burrows at the hottest times of the day. They do not have a chance to do this in a glass container standing in full sunshine. The garage or shed is also not suitable. You cannot see your pet, and the whole idea is that you should enjoy its presence. It is also too dark, too quiet and often draughty. Gerbils can cope with a temperature of 15 °C, as long as they have plenty of dry nesting material.

Once it gets colder, there is a risk of hypothermia. Gerbils like to party, but living permanently on top of a loudspeaker is too much of a good thing. Preferably place the cage in the living room, out of the sun, away from draughts and, where possible, off the ground on a (low) cupboard or table. The cage has to be closed securely, so that small children and other pets cannot open it.

Nutrition

Day-in, day-out for years on end, rodents are fed the same thing: mixed rodent food. However, research into the feeding habits of rodents in the wild has shown that they generally need a quite different and more varied diet.

Feeding in the wild

Mongolian gerbils prefer to eat herbs and herb-like plants in the wild (seeds, stems and roots). They sometimes also eat flowers and leaves. Many gerbil varieties also eat live food (insects).

Feeding in captivity

When you consider their feeding habits in the wild, it's illogical to feed gerbils only a mixture of oats, grain, barley and grass pellets all the time. These "old-fashioned" foods contain almost no animal content and thus hardly any proteins. So a lot has changed in the field of rodent foods over the last few years. Major manufacturers have developed special foods for each variety of small rodent.

Supreme petfoods, for example, makes a special gerbil food with less fat and more protein than typical hamster foods. This is available in many UK petshops.

The nutritional requirements of the gerbil are very similar to those of the hamster. Your gerbils will therefore also be very happy with a mixed hamster food. Make sure that there are not too many green grass pellets in the food. The manufacturers put all the vitamins and minerals into these green cubes, but gerbils normally do not touch them. In the wild, they hardly ever find grass, and then definitely not in a green, lush form. Whenever you buy any other food, take care that its structure is not too coarse. Rabbit food is certainly not suitable. If you use mixed rodent food, you can supplement it with dry cat or dog foods, and possibly weed or grass seeds from the bird food shelf.

Pet shops also carry ready-made foods in the form of pressed pellets. These pellets all look the same and have the same ingredients. Many breeders give their animals such foods, because then they're sure that each animal gets all the nutrition it needs. Apart from that, a lot less food is wasted as the animals don't pick out what they like best, leaving the rest. Although the feed is very comprehensive, gerbils cannot satisfy their natural urge to peel seeds. Feeding the same food every day is also very monotonous. Make sure that the food does not contain too many sunflower seeds, peanuts and other nuts. Gerbils love them, but they contain lots of fat. Your gerbils will gain weight very quickly. This is bad for their health and also causes breeding problems. You can use nuts in a very limited fashion as treats or temptation, for example when taming your pet. Scientific research has shown that gerbils eat better when they have to search for their food. Gathering their own food is a natural activity. They will completely empty a full feeding bowl put in front of them and then fill it with woodshavings. Therefore you can quite happily spread the food around the cage.

Be aware of the manufacturing date when buying food, as the vitamins are only effective for three months after manufacture. They quickly lose their power after that. Therefore, never buy too much food at once.

Just like humans, animals also love variety. Never feed your gerbil sweets, crisps, biscuits or sugar lumps. They can become very ill, as there is too much fat, salt and sugar in such food. When you want to treat your gerbil, there are plenty of healthy treats that you can add to its menu.

Vegetables and fruit

Gerbils enjoy most sorts of vegetables, but take care with them. After all, the Mongolian gerbil comes from a habitat with very little water (semi-desert) and is not used to large quantities of food with high water content. They can cause diarrhoea. Now and again your pet can be treated to a small piece of chicory, carrot, cauliflower, paprika or apple. It will enjoy most fruits, although citrus fruits are often too acid. Gerbils also enjoy dandelion, freshly cut grass and clover.

Lettuce and cabbage are best left out of their diets. These vegetables can easily cause intestinal problems. Make sure that all fresh food has been washed well (insecticides) and never gather grass, clover or dandelion from patches

Hay with herbs

next to busy roads, because of pollution. Take care to remove from the cage any pieces of fruit or vegetables that have not been eaten. There is a chance they will start to rot, which could make your gerbil ill.

Other treats

Mongolian gerbils love meal-worms, sunflower seeds and nuts. They are rich in fat and therefore not that healthy. Therefore, give them only sparsely and never feed salted nuts. Gerbils also enjoy a small piece of old bread or a raisin.

Eating droppings

Almost all rodents eat their own droppings from time to time. This is not only normal, but also necessary. During the digestion process, vitamin B12 is produced in the intestines. By eating their droppings the animals take in this important vitamin.

Young gerbils eat their parents' droppings, because they contain the bacteria they need to be able to create vitamin B12 in their own intestines during digestion.

Vitamins and minerals

Vitamins and minerals are ele-ments every body needs to stay healthy. As long as a gerbil enjoys a good, varied diet it does not need additional vitamins and minerals. These are in their food. In the chapter Your gerbil's health

there's more information about the consequences of an unbalanced diet.

Some breeders hang a so-called "mineral lick" in the cage. The animal takes in minerals by licking the stone and it seems that pregnant females, particularly, use them. Sometimes small blocks of limestone are placed in the cage. By gnawing on these the animals get extra calcium and at the same time keep their teeth sharp.

Water

Many rodents drink only small amounts of water. They come from regions where water is scar-ce and have learned to be careful with it. Some varieties can go with almost no water at all. Gerbils do, however, take in water in form of dew. It is therefore important for your gerbil to always have fresh water available. Any time it is thirsty it can drink. It is best to give water in a drinking bottle, which you hang on the outside of the cage, with the spout inside. Make sure that all animals (old and young) can reach it.

A dish of water is quickly overtur-ned or filled with sawdust or other dirt.

Behaviour

Maybe not the most obvious, but definitely the most attractive characteristic of your gerbil is its inquisitive nature. Inquisitiveness, which almost borders on meddling, as it will basically stick its nose into anything.

A gerbil will not run away and hide whenever there are sudden noises and movements. Your pet is attracted by anything new and goes to inquire before it decides whether there is danger or not. Mongolian gerbils are therefore not easily annoyed, and they only bite in exceptional cases.

Communication
Gerbils do not speak a language as people do. Although they do not talk to each other, they can still communicate. They express their feelings and intentions (such as readiness for mating) via various non-verbal signals. Gerbils are in constant contact with each other via high, squeaking sounds, which are hardly audible for human ears. Very young animals squeak a little louder. The owner

will often notice the presence of newly born young by the squeaking. Older animals, too, sometimes squeak louder. They do this when playing, but it can also be the expression of fright or sexual excitement.

Body language
The most important means of communication for gerbils are not via sounds, but through body language, which they use to express a whole range of emotions.

Alertness
A typical gerbil action is its so-called 'drumming'. The gerbil stands upright and quickly thumps on the ground with its hind legs. One of the functions of this stamping is to warn other members of the group when danger is approa-

ching. The drumming is the signal to escape or attack. Drumming is also very important during courting and mating behaviour between male and female. Young gerbils learn to drum from their parents. You can observe young gerbils imitating their parents' drumming even when there is no danger approaching.

Greeting

When gerbils greet each other, it looks like they are kissing. They lick each other's mouths, as they recognise each other by the taste of their saliva.

Happiness

Gerbils that feel at home love a good cleaning session. They wash their face, belly and paws, and clean their tail by holding it with their front paws.

Excitement

When gerbils are excited or under pressure, they jump in the air with all four feet at once. Sometimes this excited jumping is combined with boxing movements of their front paws. The boxing of two animals is often playful, but it can sometimes be very serious.

Fear

A frightened gerbil sits upright as if frozen, with its front paws folded as if it is praying.

Curiosity

A curious gerbil, too, sits upright with its front paws folded. It is, however, not as tense as a

frightened animal. It sniffs around with whiskers trembling and moves its head up and down at the same time.

Asking for a cleaning session

If your gerbil wants to be cleaned, it will roll in front of a friend and turn its head, offering its throat.

The other gerbil cannot usually resist this gesture and will gives its friend a good cleaning session.

Leave me alone

An irritated gerbil that wants to be left alone will dismiss other gerbils or your hand by pushing it away with its head.

Attacking

When gerbils are ready to fight, they box each other with their heads. Then they start a boxing and wrestling match.

Solitary or gregarious?

All animals can be put into one of two categories, depending on their behaviour towards others of their kind. Some animals live in groups, just as humans. We call these gregarious animals. These groups can have very simple structures, where the animals live next to each other, but more or less live their own lives. We see this with mice, for example. There are also animals which live in groups with very clear, strict rules. The prairie marmots, for example, have real group leaders, which are respected and obeyed by the other group members. Very often, each animal has a certain task to fulfil within the group. Most rodents are gregarious animals.

Some rodents are solitary, which means that they prefer to live on their own. They only meet up for mating in the reproduction season. The male has to make sure that it gets away quickly after the mating, as the female can injure it badly. A solitary lifestyle is often led by animals which live in dry grassland and desert areas, such as some desert mice and some special gerbils. Solitary animals often have a very strong territorial instinct. This is also obvious

with some squirrels. It is very obvious that gregarious animals are very forgiving. When observing a group of mice, you can see that they have reconciliation signals: turning the head away and/or closing the eyes. The willingness to compromise aims to prevent injuries and deaths in the group.

When an animal is willing to succumb, it is not likely to be attacked. This assumes that the animals have got enough room to escape from each other. When gregarious animals are forced to live together in a very small cage without escape options, it can cause fights. This can also happen when two gerbils that are not familiar with each other are put in one cage.

If you want to keep rodents, it is therefore very important for you to know whether your chosen animals are gregarious or solitary. A solitary rodent, which is forced to live with others, will feel constantly threatened by this situation. The animal will be unhappy and become aggressive. On the other hand, it is wrong to keep a gregarious animal on its own. It will be very unhappy and will finally pine away. In some cases, the human can replace the missing partner and offer the animal company. This might seem a nice solution, but it is not really the case: if you do not have time for your pet for a few days, it will be

It should be obvious that you should never keep a gerbil on its own. It does not only need a partner to play with, but also to scratch each other. Gerbils are just like humans in this respect: they need protection and affection.

Colony behaviour

Gregarious animals often live in colonies, which may consist of just three to eight animals, or of several thousand. Mice and rat colonies are usually very big; gerbil colonies are a little smaller. A group of Mongolian gerbils usually consists of three grown males, two to seven grown females and several young and adolescent animals. In the chapter Reproduction you will read more on mating behaviour in the colony. The colony behaviour is vitally important for the existence of the group. The members of the group build a system of burrows with nesting and storage rooms. While the group rests or looks after the young, a few members watch out or dig around a little. As soon as danger approaches, they begin to drum the ground with their back paws to warn other animals. Another function of group behaviour is to ensure a good rest. When colony animals sleep, they pile up in a heap. The youngest animals are on top. As little warmth as possible can escape, and the strongest animals protect the weak

young. In cold times, the small animals with very little body volume cannot keep themselves warm. If they were not covered by others, they would die of hypothermia. Colonies have no set pattern. Animals with a free order, such as mice and rats, constantly change their composition. With smaller (and therefore closer) colonies, this takes much longer. An alpha male of a gerbil colony therefore keeps his position for two years. He is then too old, and a younger male will take over the lead. Adolescent males cannot normally measure their strength against the adult males. They are therefore often thrown out of the group and swarm around in small bachelors' groups, until they can found their own colony. If no young females are found, the young males stay together.

House-training

In principle, most rodents are house-trained by nature. They don't like to foul their own nest and will always do their business in the same corner of their home. This can be practical because sometimes it won't be necessary to clean out the whole cage, but just to scrape out the "toilet corner".

Cuddling your gerbil

When keeping gerbils as pets, it is important that they are tame (as far as possible). This not only helps when you clean out their cage, or when they

need to be (medically) examined, but it is fun too. You can even play with them. Tame gerbils enjoy being picked up once in a while, but these little animals are not suitable to be cuddled for hours at a time; they don't like it and can get frightened and stressed. If you are looking for a cuddly animal, go to a toyshop.

Taming the gerbil

When taming a gerbil you can exploit its natural curiosity. When something unusual happens, it will run for cover, but after a while a plucky hero will reappear. Hold your hand in the cage with something tasty on it and, sooner or later, the gerbil will approach it. But don't try to catch the animal at once, because you'll destroy the newly won trust. Let the gerbil get used to the scent of your hand and wait for your gerbil to sit on it. After a few attempts, you can carefully lift your hand a little. The gerbil will get more and more comfortable with it. Never chase after your animal, it will only get frightened.

Hungry animals are easier to train with something tasty than an animal that's just eaten, so always do your taming exercises before you feed your gerbil. Taming a gerbil can sometimes require patience, so don't give up too fast if you don't get immediate results.

Shows

Hobby breeders also breed gerbils. Just like dogs, cats, rabbit, chickens and pigeons that are put on show and compete for points. Gerbil lovers have several cages with gerbils at home and try to breed particularly fine examples.

During shows, which may be one day or more, each animal is judged. A so-called "standard" exists for every known variety and colouring, which describes exactly how each variant should look. [In the UK we have different standards for more species so I have rewritten this bit]The Mongolian gerbil, and the other species can be entered in shows. During the show, an expert judge evaluates each animal in terms of size, colour, shape and condition. If you're interested in taking up this hobby you can contact a breeders' association (see the chapter on Useful Addresses)

Even if you're not planning to start breeding, but are simply interested in rodents, it's worth taking the trouble to visit a small

animal show. You can pick up a lot of information there, and often the breeders present have good animals for sale.

Colouring

The agouti is the original colour of the Mongolian gerbil. As it has been kept as a pet for a very long time and has been bred a lot, colour mutations have occurred. Today, there are several colours besides the original wild colour:

White-bellied golden agouti

The top colour is greyish brown. The hairs are slate grey near the skin, then yellow with black tips (ticking). The ticking is absent around the eyes and behind the ears. The belly is beige to white, the tail is greyish brown on the top, and underneath there is no ticking and the tuft is darker. The nails are black, as are the eyes.

Argente golden
The top colour is a warm yellow with a slate grey base. The colour is lighter around the eyes and behind the ears. The tail is like the top colour, the belly is creamy white. The nails are natural coloured and the eyes are ruby-red.

Argente cream
The fur is light beige, apricot-coloured. The base of the hairs is slate grey. The belly is white, while the nails are natural and the eyes are ruby-red.

Black
The top colour is shiny black. Belly, nails and eyes are also jet black. Sometimes, black animals have a white line on their throat, and small white lines on the front paws.

Lilac
The top colour is bluish grey with a pink sheen. Ears, paws, tail and belly are also lilac. The nails are natural, the eyes are ruby-red. Lilac animals too can have a white stripe on the throat and white stripes on the front paws.

Dove
The fur has a light grey colour, lighter than lilac. Belly, paws, ears and tail are as the top colour. The nails are natural, the eyes ruby-red.

Dark tailed white
The top colour is clear white, everywhere except for the tail. The tail can vary from light brown (a few agouti hairs) to dark brown. The nails are clear, the eyes bright red.

Pink eyed white
The whole animal is clear white, just as the Himalayan, including the tail. The eyes are bright red, the nails natural.

White bellied grey agouti
The top colour is silver-grey with black ticking. The hair base is dark slate grey. The middle colour is silver-white, the tips are black. The belly is silver-white or cream, the tail is dark on the top and lighter underneath. The eyes are black, although a red glow becomes visible when lots of light falls on them. The nails are dark natural.

Slate
This colour is exactly like black but is a dark slate grey colour. The nail colour is brownish instead of black.

Pink eyed white
The colour is off white, hardly distinguishable from clear white. Ears, tail and belly are the same colour as the rest of the gerbil. The nails are natural, the eyes are ruby-red.

Dove

Pink eyed white

Silveragouti

Birmese

White bellied cream
The fur is light cream coloured all over. The belly is white. Tail and ears are the top colour. The nails are natural, the eyes are ruby-red.

Dark eyed honey
The young dark eyed honey looks different than the adult version. Until about ten weeks, the dark eyed honey is orange-yellow coloured, with a white belly. The fur is of a lighter colour around the eyes and ears. Eyes and nails are black. There is no slate grey base. The skin at the ears, nose, genitals and on the tail is dark. As the animal gets older, the hairs on the back display black ticking. It looks as if the animal walked through coal dust. A little later the yellow colour turns more orange.

Red eyed honey
This gerbil is a yellow golden colour like an argente golden but

more yellow. The base of the hairs is white. The eyes are dark ruby, and the white belly shades up the sides of the animal.

Saffron
This gerbil looks just like an Argente Golden but the belly is yellow in stead of white. The coat also has less ticking.

Nutmeg
The younger nutmeg also looks different than the older animal. Young nutmegs have a warm orange-brown colour all over. The eyes are black and the nails are dark natural. When the gerbil is around ten weeks of age and changes its youth fur for that of the grown, it changes its colour completely. It is much darker where the new fur comes through. The new hairs have a black tic-king. This colour too can have a white stripe on the throat and white stripes on the front paws.

Silver nutmeg
This is a colouris similar to a white-bellied grey agouti when an adult, but the belly is lightly tic-ked and a creamy grey colour. When young the colour is a crea-my colour.

Burmese
The Burmese has a brown coat with almost black ears, nose, tail and paws. The eyes are black, the nails are dark natural. This colour too can have a white stripe on the

Dark eyed honey

throat and white stripes on the front paws.

Siamese
This is a lighter version of the Burmese. The top colour is cream beige and the ears, nose, tail and paws are chocolate brown. The eyes are black, but have a dark red glow. The nails are natural.

Spotted/Pied/Mottled
All gerbil colours can have white markings, although you will not see them on a white gerbil. These can take the form of spots on the head, neck and tail, or there can be flecks of white all over the body. Different patterns have different names.

New Colours
Pearl
Pearl is the agouti form of the Burmese. It is a very light white-bellied grey agouti with the tail of the wild colour. In the rabbit world, this colour is called chinchilla medium. It comes also in a grey form. The grey form is preferred by many breeders.

Schimmel
Young schimmel look like the dark eyed honey. From about ten weeks of age the animals develop completely differently: they become lighter. They become constantly lighter on the body, only the base stays yellow. A spot on the forehead is the last to lighten up. The coat around the ears, nose

Argente Golden

and genitals is dark, the eyes are black. The nails are very light natural. There is also a red-eyed form without dark ears, nose and genitals.

Polarfox
The polarfox has a youth coat, which is different from that of the grown animal. The young polarfox is creamy white, with black eyes and natural nails. The skin around the nose, ears, genitals and on the tail is dark. Grown animals have a light ticking over the top colour.

Blue
A new and very rare colour is exactly like a black, but the fur is a dark blueish grey instead of black.

Black eyed white
This gerbil is a light cream colour with a small amount of black or grey ticking. It has almost black eyes.

Polar

Reproductio

Of course it is nice to breed a litter of gerbils, but you need to be sure in advance whether the young have a good home to go to, because they must be separated from the mother in six weeks or so.

Pale gerbil with young

You can ask your pet shop whether they need young gerbils or perhaps neighbours, friends or acquaintances will take them.

Should you be left with young, then you must find another way of housing them, because they really must not be kept in the cage with their mother. One solution, of course, is to go out and buy several more cages as homes for the youngsters, but this is not an option for many people. So only start to breed if you've found good homes for the young!

Male or female

To breed gerbils, you first need to be sure that you have a male and a female available. With gerbils, the difference between the sexes cannot be seen at a

glance. You have to examine them closely under the tail.

As with most rodents, you can tell the sex of a gerbil from the space between its anus and its genital opening. This distance is much larger on males than on females. On grown males you can also easily see the shape of the scrotum.

Fertility

Gerbils are fertile at about three months of age. As pregnancy takes approximately 24 days, healthy couples can have their first young at the age of four months. It is advisable not to mate a female gerbil before five to six months of age, as she needs all her energy for growing in the first few months. A female gerbil can have young up to an age of fourteen to twenty months. Her most fertile age is around her first birthday. Beforehand and afterwards, she will have fewer and smaller litters. One female will raise approximately seven litters in her life. There are generally four to five young in one litter, but there can be up to ten. If a gerbil has given birth to so many young, she will be less fertile for a while after the birth. This is a natural protection to allow her to recover. Females can be mated immediately after an average litter. This is also no problem, as suckling her young delays the next birth. When the new babies are born after four weeks, the older ones are already approaching independence.

In-breeding

To breed responsibly, you must only ever use strong, healthy adult animals. And you may never put any male together with any female, because there is a high risk of in-breeding. For instance, if you've been given a brother and sister from a neighbour's litter, it's better not to breed them. Pairing these animals together is a serious form of in-breeding, and who can guarantee that your neighbour's litter was not also the result of pairing a brother and sister? Most rodents live in fairly isolated groups in the wild. Scientists wondered whether this life does not automatically lead to multiple in-breeding. In-breeding means that a female mates with a relative (father, bro-

Female

Male

ther, uncle or nephew). In-breeding is harmful, because the same genetic information appears several times in diluted form. The animals do not only appear increasingly similar, but they also develop a one-sided character. In practice, animals become smaller, less fertile and vulnerable to illnesses and hereditary disorders through in-breeding (or very selective breeding). Scientific research has shown that in-breeding hardly ever occurs in wild gerbil populations. Females in season leave the colony to mate with males from a colony nearby. Then they return to their own group to give birth and raise the young with the help of their uncles and aunts.

Pairing

When the time has come for a litter, you have to bring male and female together. This is called 'pairing'. In the wild, the partners can choose each other and they have plenty of room available. This is completely different in captivity. The owner chooses the partners and puts them in a relatively small space (the cage). Normally the pairing runs smoothly. It is advisable to provide plenty of shelter in the cage, so the partners can escape from each other, if necessary. You can fill the whole cage with a thick layer of fresh hay and a number of tins and toilet rolls. Always put the female into the male's cage, and never vice versa! If the coupling

is not successful this way, you can put the female into a small show cage. These cages are approximately ten by fifteen centimetres and are available in most pet shops. Put the cage (with a well fitting lid) into the male's cage on its side, so that the animals can see

and smell each other through the lid. They can even act aggressively towards one another, but they cannot injure each other. After about 24 hours, you can let the two animals together. This will normally go without problems.

Mating

A female is ready for mating when she is at a certain point in her cycle. She is in season only in this one phase (the oestrus). The season occurs once in four to six days and lasts for about twelve hours. Male gerbils normally only

try to mate with females when they are in season. A complex foreplay proceeds the actual covering (which normally happens in the evening). The animals chase each other around, and drum with their paws once in a while. They also smell each other's genitals. When the female is ready, she stands still and lifts her backend, so that the male can mount her. Gerbils mate quickly (less than half a minute), but often. The male has to penetrate the female approximately ten times before he ejaculates. He cleans his genitals after each penetration. The female only cleans herself after the ejaculation.

Pregnancy and birth

It is not always easy to spot a pregnancy. It is sometimes obvious that the female has become fatter, but in some cases she does not at all. Your gerbil will be just as active during pregnancy as before. She will withdraw discretely for delivery. The newly born young are not yet fully developed. They are naked, deaf, toothless and their eyes are closed. They weigh approximately two grams and are three centimetres long. The young are bigger in small litters. The babies are completely helpless in this first stage. They can only squeak when they are hungry or cold, in the hope that their mother will quickly come to help. The first few days after birth are critical. The weak animals

usually die during this time. It is advisable to feed the mother extra protein, for example with dry cat food or mealworms. You can judge by their stomachs whether the young have been fed sufficiently. If it is filled with milk, the stomach looks like a white bean under the abdominal skin.

The first few weeks

The father, too, helps with the care of the young, especially when they start to crawl around the nest after approximately ten days. He helps the mother to bring them back. They do this by carefully carrying the young in their mouths. The father also keeps the nest warm. When the young are two to three days old, the ears begin to develop. The first growth of hair becomes visible a few days later. Gerbils grow quickly. At ten days old, they will try to crawl out of the nest. Their eyes open shortly after the seventeenth day. This is when they also start to try solid food. After about 24 days, they are no longer fed by their mother, but eat solid food.
In very exceptional cases, the parents eat their young. They do not do this because they are hungry, but because the young are not viable or already dead. The gerbils follow their instinct and keep the nest clean in this way.

Pallid gerbil takes her young in her mouth to bring it back to the nest

Other species

The Mongolian gerbil has been known and loved as a pet for years. However, there are about eighty other species of gerbil.

Cheesman gerbil
(*Gerbillus cheesmani*)
with a typical
gerbilllus-build

A number of them are closely related to the Mongolian and are also suitable as pets. As there are only a very small number of them in captivity, the populations need to be managed very carefully.

Collaboration between owners of other species can ensure that the numbers are carefully expanded, so that more enthusiasts can enjoy these lovely animals. The very sparse and often difficult to access, information on the care of these special breeds should increase and become more accessible with increasing knowledge about these animals. In general, feeding, care and housing do not differ much between the Mongolian gerbil and the other species. In this chapter you will get an overview of the different gerbil species and

their genera. To prevent misunderstandings between scientists and friends, Latin names are used all over the world. Ask a gerbil fan in Russia about a gerbil, and he will not know what you are talking about. He will know Meriones unguiculatus, however! The animal's genus is always indicated by the first part of the Latin name, for example Meriones. The second part indicates the species: unguiculatus. If there is a sub-species, it is indicated by a third part. If a certain term appears several times in a text, it is written out once, and then abbreviated: M. unguiculatus.

Meriones species

The tribe Meriones not only consists of the Mongolian gerbil (*M. unguiculatus*), but also its nearest relatives, often called "jirds".

They live mostly in the semi-desert and the steppes of Central Asia, a biotope where temperatures drop below freezing in winter. The Meriones species all form large colonies. The Sundevall's jird (*M. crassus*) is a particularly friendly animal that is at home in an area from North Africa to Afghanistan and Pakistan. Sundevall's jirds have such a tame nature that even wild animals do not bite when taken out of their burrows. Their head has an obvious triangular shape. They have a thick woolly coat which makes them appear bigger than the Mongolian gerbil. The Shaw's jird (*M. shawi*) is the most common gerbil species after the Mongolian Gerbil in the United Kingdom. They are less social than Mongolian gerbils, but a pair will normally live together. They are very friendly towards humans, and being nearly twice as long as a Mongolian Gerbil, they are easy to handle. The Libyan jird *(M. libycus)* is not known in the United Kingdom, but some people

Sundevall jird
(Meriones crassus)

Libyan jird
(Meriones lybicus)
with a typical
Meriones-build

Other species

Libyan jird
(*M. lybicus*)

Breed	Body length	Tail length
Mongolian gerbil	11 - 13.5	9.5 - 10.5
Sundevall's jird	10 - 12.5	7.8 - 11.4
Shaw's jird	ca. 14	ca. 14
Libyan jird	13 - 15	14 - 15
Persian jird	13 - 17	14 - 19
Cheesman's gerbil	ca. 10	ca. 12
Pallid gerbil	ca. 10.7	ca. 13.7
Duprasi gerbil	ca. 10	ca. 5
Bushy-tailed jird	10 - 13	13 - 16

Thomas jird
(*Meriones thomasi)*

think that most of the Shaw's jirds in the country are hybrid animals – half Shaw's jird, and half Libyan jird. This is because Shaw's jirds have lived in the United Kingdom for nearly twenty years and carry many features of both species. They also behave differently to Shaw's jirds bred in other countries, and from Shaw's jirds captured in the wild. The Persian jird *(M. periscus)* is one of the largest gerbils kept as pets in Western Europe. It is an attractive animal but needs lots of room. A distinctive characteristic is the big eyes, as the Persian jird is more nocturnal.

The Gerbillus species

The whole gerbil sub-family *(Gerbillinae)* owes its name to the Gerbillus genus. The animals belonging to this tribe are all called gerbils or dipodils, rather than jirds. They differ widely in build and occurrence from the jirds (Meriones). Gerbillus species are much slimmer, have longer back legs and are more yellow-orange in colour. Their burrows tend to be more simpleburrow. These animals are not strictly solitary or gregarious, but this varies: sometimes they live in groups of various sizes, sometimes they live on their own. The most common Gerbillus species to be found in the United Kingdom are Cheesman's gerbil *(G. cheesmani)* and The Pallid gerbil *(G. perpallidus)*. The two species look so very much alike

that it is very difficult to tell the difference. They are both active, affectionate animals that are easy to handle. Their care is very much like that of the Mongolian gerbil, with the difference that the number of males in a group has to be smaller than the number of females. Other Gerbillus species are sometimes available from specialist breeders.

Other tribes

There are other gerbil tribes besides *Meriones* and *Gerbillus*. This book is not thick enough to discuss all the tribes in detail. Here are a few more important varieties:

The Fat Tailed gerbil

(Pachyuromys duprasi), sometimes just called "Duprasi" is the most friendly of all the gerbils. Even when caught in the wild, these animals can be taken out of the trap with bare hands. They do not bite. It owes its name to its tail, which the Duprasi gerbil uses to store fat for times of famine.

The Bushy-tailed jird *(Skeetamys calures)* is an attractive, active gerbil with a bushy 'squirrel-tail'. It has a long, dark-brown coat.

Pallid gerbil
(Gerbillus perpallides)

Fet tailed gerbil
(Pachuromys duprasi)

Taterillus emini

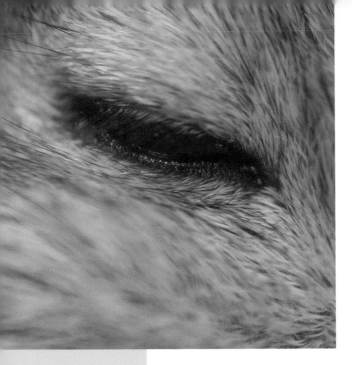

Your gerbil's health

Fortunately, gerbils generally have few health problems. A healthy example has bright eyes and is lively. Its coat is smooth, soft and regular. Its rear end is dry and clean. A sick gerbil sits withdrawn all the time.

Its coat is dull and stands open, as if wet. The animal's back is raised, even when walking.

Prevention

The rule that "prevention is better than a cure" also applies to small animals such as the gerbil. It's not always easy to cure a sick gerbil. They are so small that even a vet doesn't always know how to treat them.

Even a light cold can prove fatal for a gerbil and the biggest risks to its health are draughts and damp.

There are a few general rules that you can follow if your gerbil is ill:

- Keep the animal in a quiet semi-dark place. Stress, crowding and noise won't help it get better.
- Keep the animal warm, but make sure its surroundings are not too hot. The best temperature is 20 to 21 °C.
- Don't wait too long before visiting a vet. Small rodents that get sick usually die within a few days.
- The patient should always have fresh water and remember that your animal may be too weak to reach its water bottle.
- Sick animals often eat little or nothing. Give it a small piece of apple or other fruit.
- Several of the conditions mentioned below can spread very easily. Do not separate gerbils that live together as they will have already been exposed to the relevant agent, however, if you have more than one tank or cage,

always make sure you do not carry the infection from one group of gerbils to the other.

Colds and pneumonia

Draughts are the most common cause of colds and pneumonia for gerbils, so choose the place for its home carefully.

They can withstand low temperatures, but cold in combination with a draught almost inevitably leads to a cold. The gerbil starts sneezing and gets a wet nose. If its cold gets worse, the animal starts to breathe with a rattling sound and its nose will run even more, so it's now time to visit the vet, who can prescribe antibiotics. A gerbil with a cold or pneumonia must be kept in a draught-free and warm room (22 to 25 °C).

Diarrhoea

Diarrhoea is another formidable threat to gerbils and often ends fatally. Unfortunately, diarrhoea is usually the result of incorrect feeding, sometimes in combination with draughts or damp. Most cases of diarrhoea are caused by giving the animal food with too high a moisture content. After all,

the gerbil's digestive system is not used to it. Rotten food or dirty drinking water can also be a cause. You can do a lot to prevent diarrhoea yourself.

Should your gerbil become a victim then you must take any moist food out of the cage immediately. Feed your animal only dry bread, boiled rice or crispbread. Replace its water with lukewarm camomile tea. Clean out its cage litter and nest material twice a day.

If your gerbil is not better within one to two days, you must take it to the vet's! Once the diarrhoea is over, you need to disinfect the whole cage.

Wet tail
E-coli bacteria causes an especially serious form of diarrhoea and most victims die within 48 hours. Gerbils that fall victim to this disease have a constantly wet tail and anus; they won't eat and become apathetic.

E-coli bacteria are normally present in small quantities in the intestines of a small rodent. In the event of reduced resistance or stress, the bacteria suddenly becomes active. Whenever your gerbil has a wet tail take it to the vet's immediately. The other animals in the cage also have to be treated. As this disease is highly contagious, you have to pay particular attention to hygiene.

Tumours
In contrast to most other rodents, gerbils seldom have problems with tumours, and when they do it is mostly in old age. Tumours occur more frequently in strains where in-breeding has occurred, in other words where animals have been crossed with their own family members. The most common tumours affect the female's teats, but tumours can also be the result of skin cancer. These forms can be operated on but, because of the animal's age, this rarely makes sense.

Another form of tumour is caused by an infection under the skin and is called an abscess. A small wound may heal, but an infection remains under the skin. This type of tumour can be easily treated by the vet who opens and cleans it. Should your gerbil show signs of a tumour, take it straight to the vet's. Delaying can only make things worse, both with skin cancer and abscesses.

Bite wounds
The most common injuries suffered by a gerbil are the result of fights. Pairing adult animals is not always easy and can sometimes result in fierce fighting.

Bite wounds generally heal quickly, and as long as they're not too big or too deep you usually don't need to do much. Don't let the wounded animal sit on sawdust or sand for the first few days. Small pieces might get into the wound. Shredded paper or kitchen roll is a good alternative.

Broken bones

Gerbils sometimes break bones because they get stuck with their paws, jump off your hand or fall from a table. An animal with a broken paw will not put weight on it and will limp around the cage.

If it's a "straight" fracture (the paw is not deformed), this will heal within a few weeks. Take care that the gerbil can reach its food and drink without difficulty. If a gerbil has broken its back, it's best to have it put to sleep. If in doubt about a possible fracture, always see your vet.

Broken teeth

Gerbils that are fed an unbalanced diet with too few minerals run the risk of broken teeth. If you notice that your gerbil has a broken tooth, check that its diet is properly balanced. The vet can prescribe gistocal tablets to restore the calcium level. A broken front tooth will normally grow back, but you should check regularly that this is happening.

Overgrown teeth

A rodent's front teeth grow continuously and are ground down regularly by its gnawing. A genetic defect, a heavy blow or lack of gnawing opportunities can disrupt this process. Its teeth are ground irregularly and in the end don't fit together properly. In some cases the teeth continue to grow unchecked, even into the opposite jaw.

When a rodent's teeth are too long, it can no longer chew properly and the animal will lose weight and eventually starve to death.

Long teeth can easily be clipped back. A vet can show you how to do that, or do it for you if you don't feel able. Take care that your rodent always has enough to gnaw on. A piece of breeze block, a block of wood or a branch will do fine.

Malnutrition ailments

Not only calcium deficiency, but also a shortage of other minerals and vitamins can lead to sicknesses. See the table on page 58 for an overview of sicknesses that can arise from certain deficiencies.

A healthy coat

It is very important that your gerbil's coat is kept in very good condition. This prevents the animals from becoming infested with parasites and other problems. Gerbils look after their coat by bathing in the wild - not in water, but in sand. They roll in the sand, which gets between their hairs and absorbs all the grease and dirt. After their bath they shake themselves, so that the dirt leaves the coat with the sand. In this way, the coat remains untangled and aired, and therefore offers ideal insulation. Not all gerbil breeds need sand baths. Some hardly ever use it, others really need it. Mongolian gerbils really love to take such a bath, and it is always a very attractive show to watch. You should offer them the opportunity to enjoy themselves once in a while. Shell sand or special bathing sand for chinchillas is ideal. Shell sand is most often used in birdcages and consists of silver sand mixed with pieces of shells and aniseeds. Gerbils love the seeds and sometimes even eat the shells to fulfil their need for calcium. The chinchilla sand is made of ground clay and is available in different structures, from fine to coarse. A disadvantage is that chinchilla sand is fairly expensive, but you can solve this problem by mixing it with shell sand. If the sand has remained dry during the bath, you can sieve it through and use it again. You have to replace it after the third time. When it is bathing time, put a bowl with sand into the cage. The animals will go for the sand straight away. Remove the sand after the bath. If you leave it in, the gerbils will dig and root until all the sand is mixed into the bedding and the nesting material.

Parasites

Parasites are small creatures that live at the cost of their host. The best known are fleas on dogs and cats. Rodents seldom have problems with parasites, and certainly not healthy animals. Weak, sick or poorly cared for animals, however, are far more likely to be affected. You mostly discover parasites only when an animal starts to scratch itself and gets bald patches. If you notice that your gerbil is itching and scratches itself frequently, then it's probably suffering from mites (tiny relatives of spiders some of which feed on blood). These mites are often spread by birds, and gerbils sometimes pick up a flea from a dog or cat.

A pet shop or vet can advise you on dealing with parasites. Remedies sold for bird mites are often effective.

Skin mites

The skin mite is a particularly harmful parasite. Fortunately they seldom occur but if they affect your gerbil, you will have to treat it. The skin mite is a minute spiderlike creature that creeps into its host's skin, making the mite itself almost never visible. It causes scabs and eczema, known as scabies, which sometimes covers the whole skin within a month. Skin mites are infectious and can be passed on to other animals. Your vet or a good pet shop will have treatments for skin mites.

Read the instructions on the packaging thoroughly. In most cases the infected animal must be bathed in the substance. Dry your gerbil off well to prevent it catching a cold and put it in a warm place (minimum 25 °C).

Fungal skin infections

Rodents can sometimes suffer from fungal skin infections, which cause small areas of flaking in the ears or nose. This is known as ringworm, and is caused by the same fungus as athelete's foot. Skin fungi are infectious to humans and animals but easy to treat. But don't let the problem go on for too long because the animal may suffer other ailments because of it. Your vet has standard medicines against fungi, although atheletes foot powder can be just as effective. Treatment may take a long time, several weeks, to make sure the fungus has been completely eradicated.

Old age

Obviously we hope that your gerbil will grow old without disease and pain. However gerbils live nowhere near as long as humans and you must accept that after a couple of years you have an aging gerbil to care for. An old gerbil will slowly become quieter and get some grey hair in its coat but can still live an active and happy life.

Deficiency of	Symptoms	Found in
Protein	Poor coat, hair loss, pneumonia, infertility and poor growth of young animals, aggression (both with too much and too little)	Peas, beans, soy, cheese
Vitamin A	Pneumonia, damage to mucous membrane or eyes, growth problems, diarrhea and general infections, cramps, small litters	Root vegetables, egg yolk, fresh greens, bananas and other fruit, cheese
Vitamin B complex	Hair loss, reduced fertility, weight loss, trembling, nervous symptoms, anemia, infections	Oat flakes, greens, fruit, clover, dog biscuits, grains
Vitamin C	The Guinea Pig produces this itself, deficiency rarely a problem	Greens, fruit
Vitamin D	Growth problems, poor bone condition. Too much vitamin D causes calcium loss in bones and calcium deposits in blood vessels	Dairy products, egg-yolk
Vitamin E	Infertility, muscle infections, nervous problems, bleeding and poor growth of young animals	Egg yolk, sprouting grains, fresh grains, greens
Vitamin K	(Nose) bleeding, poor healing of wounds and growth problems. Normally produced in the animal's intestines.	Greens
Calcium	Lameness, calcium loss in bones and broken teeth	Mineral preparations, dairy products, varied diet
Potassium	Weight loss, heart problems and ascitis, wetness in open abdominal cavity	Fruit
Sodium	Can only occur with serious diarrhea	Cheese, varied diet
Magnesium	Restlessness, irritability, cramps, diarrhea and hair loss	Greens, grains
Iron	Anemia, stomach and intestinal disorders, infertility	Greens, grains, meat
Iodine	Metabolic disorders and thyroid gland abnormalities	Greens, grains, water

Tips for the gerbil

- Draughts and dampness are the biggest threat to your gerbil's health.
- Be aware of in-breeding, especially when breeding other species of gerbils.
- Offer your gerbils a sand bath once in a while. They love it and it is good for their coat.
- Gerbils are gregarious animals. A gerbil on its own will be very unhappy!
- Remove rotting food from the cage. It can cause illness.
- Never feed your gerbils too much fresh food. It causes diarrhoea.
- Gerbils love to dig and root. Toilet rolls and cardboard boxes make great toys.
- If your gerbil is suffering from a contagious disease, put it in quarantine.

- Have a look round a small animal show.
- Never transport a gerbil in a cardboard box: it has very sharp teeth.
- Even though gerbils are very economic with water: they always need to have fresh water available.
- Buying a gerbil has to be properly considered.
- A gerbil is not a toy. If you want a cuddly toy, go to a toy shop.

The gerbil on the internet

If you want to know more about gerbils than you have read in this book, there are several places to look. Besides reading books, you can have a look on the internet. Several gerbil fans have constructed information sites. Part of this book, too, has come from a special web page: www.gerbil-info.com by Karin van Veen.

You can also look at the following addresses:
http://www.gerbils.co.uk
http://home.wtal.de/her/gerbils/colors.htm
http://netvet.wustl.edu/species/gerbils/GERBILS.TXT
http://www.gerbilshowsuk.org
http://members.nanc.com/~mhaines/gerbil.html
http://www.gerbilsanonymous.com/

You can find links to other pages from these.

www.gerbils.co.uk
The National Gerbil Society is a British society for the promotion of Gerbils and Jirds as pets, and exhibition animals.

www.smallandfurries.co.uk
For people who like rodents more than is actually healthy for them. Contains information on the species, various articles, links, massage board and more.

www.maisel.de/~eva/cages.html
1001 Ideas About How to House Gerbils.

http://agsgerbils.org
The American Gerbil Society is dedicated to promoting interest in these wonderful pets, as well as supporting the responsible breeding of the species through shows in which gerbils compete.

www.geocities.com/heartland/park/6961/index.html
Find out what kind of colour your gerbil has with the use of the Color Chart for the Mongolian Gerbil.

www.gerbilworld.co.uk/
On this site there is information on Gerbils e.g. Housing, Gerbil Care etc. There are also pictures of Gerbils and links to other sites.

www.gerbilshowsuk.org/
Rodent House is a small mammal stud based in Manchester, UK. Its main function is a conservation breeding program for Mongolian gerbils and their coat colours, and also for the present UK captive bred Gerbil Species. On this site you can find lot's of information on gerbils.

www.mypetstop.com
An international, multilingual website with information on keeping, breeding, behavior, health related issues and much more.

www.aboutpets.info
The website of the publisher of the About Pets book series. An overview of the titles, availability in which languages and where in the world the books are sold.

National Gerbil Society

National Gerbil Society

The National Gerbil Society (previously known as The National Mongolian Gerbil Society) is a British society for the promotion of Gerbils and Jirds as pets, and exhibition animals. Overseas members are invited. It was founded in 1970. All members receive:

- A quarterly journal, sent by post containing the latest gerbil news, show reports, articles, member's letters and information on gerbil care.
- A Yearbook giving the rules, show regulations and breed standards.

Members can exhibit at one of our shows held in various parts of Great Britain. At our shows exhibitors compete for trophies and rosettes. Most importantly our shows are fun and give our members an opportunity to meet others who keep and breed gerbils.

National Gerbil Society

373 Lynmouth Ave
MORDEN
Surrey
SM4 4RY

Tel: 020 8241 8942
E-mail: jackie@gerbils.co.uk
http://www.gerbils.co.uk

The Mongolian gerbil

Latin name:	*Meriones unguiculatus*
Discovered by:	Milne-Edwards, 1867
Tribe:	Gerbillinae
Origin:	Mongolia
Lifestyle:	gregarious
Rhythm of life:	active daytime, dusk and night
Body length:	110- 135 mm
Tail length:	95- 105 mm
Weight:	60- 85 grams
Body temperature:	38.4 degrees °C
Fertility:	48 days onwards
Pregnancy:	24- 43 days
Number of young:	4- 12
Birth weight:	approximately 3 grams
Eyes open:	16- 20 days
Lactation:	21- 28 days
Life expectancy:	4 years

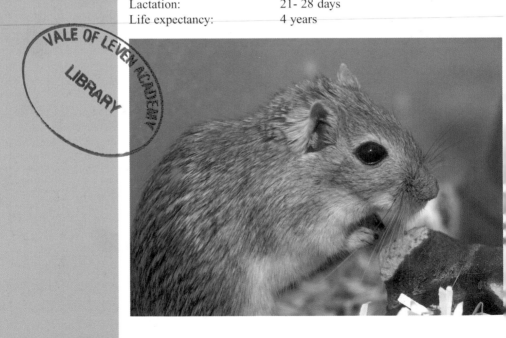